THE SERVICE OF THE
ANOINTING OF THE SICK

The Service of the Anointing of the Sick

translated by

Paul Meyendorff

ST VLADIMIR'S SEMINARY PRESS
CRESTWOOD, NEW YORK
2009

Library of Congress Cataloging-in-Publication Data

Orthodox Eastern Church.
[Euchelaion, English]
The service of the anointing of the sick / translated by Paul Meyendorff.
  p. cm.
Companion to: The anointing of the sick.
ISBN 978-0-88141-242-0
  1. Unction—Liturgy—Texts.   2. Orthodox Eastern Church—
Liturgy—Texts.   I. Title.
BX375.E73A45 2009
264'.019087—dc22

2009010141

ST VLADIMIR'S SEMINARY PRESS
575 Scarsdale Rd, Crestwood, NY 10707
1-800-204-2665
www.svspress.com

ISBN 978-0-88141-242-0

PRINTED IN THE UNITED STATES OF AMERICA

CONTENTS

INTRODUCTION 7

The Rite of Anointing of the Sick 11

An Abbreviated Rite of Anointing 71

Introduction

Is any among you suffering? Let him pray. Is any cheerful? Let him sing praise. Is any among you sick? Let him call for the elders of the church, and let them pray over him, anointing him with oil in the name of the Lord; and the prayer of faith will save the sick man, and the Lord will raise him up; and if he has committed sins, he will be forgiven. Therefore confess your sins to one another, and pray for one another, that you may be healed. (Jas 5.13–16)

Healing is too important to be left solely to the medical profession. Yet that is exactly what our modern society has done. The sick are herded into large hospitals, hooked up to an ever-increasing array of machines, and pumped full of wonder drugs. Using modern technology, physicians are now able to prolong "life" almost indefinitely. Many once-deadly diseases have been eliminated or become curable. Physical pain can be controlled, if not totally eliminated. A vast, impersonal medical bureaucracy, controlled by doctors, governments, and insurance companies, has arisen, reaching deep into the life (and pockets) of every individual.

Yet this remarkable medical progress comes with a price. Sickness and dying have become the responsibility of a medical establishment which treats humans merely as mechanisms that have broken down and need repair (or are beyond repair). The sick are removed from their homes, separated from their families, jobs, churches—from society. Their bodies are invaded, poked and probed as physicians and other health professionals perform their duties. But who is to care for their emotional and spiritual well-being? In recent years, hospitals have hired increasing numbers of social workers and chaplains, but these are very much junior partners in the medical enterprise, often barely tolerated by the "professionals." Doctors remain very much the "high priests" of the medical system we have created for ourselves.

As a society, we have chosen to leave healing to the medical profession. Doctors and hospitals have all the knowledge and technology, and we are perfectly happy to leave everything in their hands. Our consciences are clear when we provide our loved ones—our parents, our spouses, our children—with the best medical care that money can buy.

Hospitals, nursing homes and long-term care facilities not only provide medical care, but also insulate the rest of us from having to come face-to-face with pain, suffering and death, and with our own mortality. "Leave it to the professionals," we say, "that's their job." Rationalizing in this way, we keep sickness out of sight, out of mind; we postpone facing the reality of sickness and death as long as possible, until we must each face it on our own, unprepared as we are.

As a result, while we may be very good at addressing the physical aspects of sickness, we altogether neglect its spiritual side. Yet the spiritual suffering which accompanies physical illness can often be far worse than any physical pain. Separation from family and church, guilt, the anxiety caused by facing one's mortality, the loss of control over one's life—all these can be sources of ago-

nizing pain. Writing in the nineteenth century, Leo Tolstoy
described the agonizing suffering endured by Ivan Ilich, a well-to-
do provincial judge:

> The doctor said that his physical suffering was terrible, and
> that was true; but more terrible than his physical suffering
> was his spiritual suffering, and in this lay his chief agony . . .
>
> He lay down on his back and began to pass his life in
> review in an entirely new fashion . . . He saw himself, all that
> he had been living by, and saw clearly all that was not right,
> that it was all a terrible, huge deception, which concealed
> both life and death. This consciousness increased, multiplied
> tenfold his physical sufferings.[1]

This pain the medical doctors could not cure. True healing, which
is both physical and spiritual, can be given only by Christ, who is
the "Physician of our souls and bodies."

This healing ministry of Christ is a primary task of the
Church, which is the presence of Christ in this sick and fallen
world. We are Christ's presence in the world and we, as the
Church, are charged with bringing healing to those around us. At
the Last Judgment, we shall have to answer whether we "fed the
poor, welcomed the stranger, clothed the naked, visited the sick
. . ." (Matt 25.31–46). Our contemporary church life is sorely
lacking in this regard. Few parishes encourage their members to
engage in this ministry, which is often simply forgotten or left up
to the priest alone. Few communities make full and appropriate

---

[1]Leo Tolstoy, *The Death of Ivan Ilich* (vol. 9 of The Collected Works;
trans. Leo Wiener; New York: Willey Book Company, 1904), 75–6.

use of the sacrament of healing, the anointing of the sick. We do not even make this ministry of healing available to our own parishioners, or to members of our own families, who are all too often left to suffer and die alone, in hospitals and nursing homes. For this we shall be held accountable.

The present volume contains a new translation of the text of the full service of anointing, conveniently formatted for liturgical use by both clergy and faithful. It contains as well an abbreviated version suitable for use in a hospital room or at home, for whenever performing the full rite may not be possible. It is my fervent hope that, through this effort, the anointing of the sick will regain the prominent place it deserves in parish life. Those interested in looking deeper into the meaning of the rite should consult my study, published simultaneously with this edition of the service, entitled *The Anointing of the Sick*.[2]

Paul Meyendorff
Fr Alexander Schmemann Professor of Liturgical Theology
St Vladimir's Orthodox Theological Seminary

---

[2]Paul Meyendorff, *The Anointing of the Sick* (Orthodox Liturgy Series 1; Crestwood, NY: SVS Press, 2009).

The Rite of Anointing of the Sick

The Service of Holy Oil, Sung by Seven Priests Assembled in a Church, or in a House

A small table is prepared, and on it is placed a bowl of wheat and a gospel book. An empty vigil lamp is set on the wheat, and seven cotton swabs for anointing are stuck into the wheat surrounding the lamp. Two containers, one with olive oil, the other with water (or red wine), are also placed next to it. Seven presbyters stand around the table, vested in epitrachilia and phelonia and holding candles. The senior priest incenses three times around the table, then the entire church or house, and the people. Then he stands before the table, facing east, and begins, saying:

PRIEST: Blessed is our God, always, now and ever, and unto ages of ages.

READER: Amen. Holy God, Holy Mighty, Holy Immortal, have mercy on us. (3) Glory to the Father, and to the Son, and to the Holy Spirit, now and ever and unto ages of ages. Amen. O most holy Trinity, have mercy on us. Lord, cleanse us from our sins. Master, pardon our transgressions. Holy One, visit and heal our infirmities for your name's sake.

Lord, have mercy. (3)

Our Father, who art in heaven, hallowed be thy name. Thy kingdom come. Thy will be done, on earth as it is in heaven. Give us this day our daily bread; and forgive us our trespasses, as we forgive those who trespass against us; and lead us not into temptation, but deliver us from evil.

 For yours is the kingdom, and the power, and the glory, of the Father, and of the Son, and of the Holy Spirit, now and ever, and unto ages of ages.

 Amen. Lord, have mercy. (12)

Glory to the Father, and to the Son, and to the Holy Spirit, now and ever, and unto ages of ages. Amen.

Come, let us worship God our King. Come, let us worship and fall down before Christ, our King and our God. Come, let us worship and fall down before the very Christ, our King and our God.

Psalm 143[142]

Hear my prayer, O Lord; give ear to my supplications! In your faithfulness answer me, in your righteousness! Enter not into judgment with your servant; for no man living is righteous before you. For the enemy has pursued me; he has crushed my life to the ground; he has made me sit in darkness like those long dead. Therefore my spirit faints within me; my heart within me is appalled. I remember the days of old, I meditate on all that you have done; I muse on what your hands have wrought. I stretch out my hands to you; my soul thirsts for you like a parched land. Make haste to answer me, O Lord! My spirit fails! Hide not your face from me, lest I be like those who go down to the pit. Let me hear in the morning of your steadfast love, for in you I put my trust. Teach me the way I should go, for to you I lift up my soul. Deliver me, O Lord, from my enemies! I have fled to you for refuge! Teach me to do your will, for you are my God! Let your good Spirit lead me on a level path! For your name's sake, O Lord, preserve my life! In your righteousness bring me out of trouble! And in your steadfast love cut off my enemies, and destroy all my adversaries, for I am your servant.

Glory to the Father, and to the Son, and to the Holy Spirit, now and ever, and unto ages of ages. Amen.

Alleluia, alleluia, alleluia, glory to you, O God. (3)

And the deacon recites the little litany:

DEACON: Again and again, in peace, let us pray to the Lord.

PEOPLE: Lord, have mercy.

DEACON: Help us, save us, have mercy on us, and protect us, O God, by your grace.

PEOPLE: Lord, have mercy.

DEACON: Remembering our most holy, pure, most blessed and glorious Lady, the Theotokos and ever-virgin Mary, with all the saints, let us commit ourselves, and one another, and our whole life, to Christ our God.

PEOPLE: To you, O Lord.

PRIEST: For to you belong all glory, honor, and worship: to the Father and the Son and the Holy Spirit, now and ever, and unto ages of ages.

PEOPLE: Amen.

And the Alleluia is sung in tone 6:

DEACON: Alleluia, alleluia, alleluia.

PEOPLE: Alleluia, alleluia, alleluia.

DEACON, *verse:* O Lord, rebuke me not in your anger, nor chasten me in your wrath. (Ps 6.1)

 Alleluia, alleluia, alleluia.

 verse: Be gracious to me, O Lord, for I am languishing. (Ps 6.2)

PEOPLE: Alleluia, alleluia, alleluia.

Then the troparia are sung:

Have mercy on us, O Lord, have mercy on us. For we sinners, void of all defense, offer to you, as to our Master, this petition: Have mercy on us.

Glory . . .

Have mercy on us, O Lord, for in you have we trusted, and do not be very angry with us, nor remember our iniquities. But look down even now on us, for you are of tender compassion, and deliver us from our enemies. For you are our God, and we are your people. We are all the work of your hand, and we call on your name.

Now and ever . . .

Open to us the door of your loving-kindness, O blessed Theotokos. Because we have set our hope on you, may we not fail, but through you may we be delivered from all adversities: for you are the salvation of all Christians.

Then the reader chants Psalm 51[50]:

Psalm 51[50]

Have mercy on me, O God, according to your steadfast love; according to your abundant mercy blot out my transgressions. Wash me thoroughly from my iniquity, and cleanse me from my sin! For I know my transgressions, and my sin is ever before me. Against you only have I sinned, and done that which is evil in your sight, so that you are justified in your sentence and blameless in your judgment. Behold, I was brought forth in iniquities, and in sins did my mother bear me. Behold, you desire truth in the inward being; therefore teach me wisdom in my secret heart. Purge me with hyssop, and I shall be clean; wash me, and I shall be whiter than snow. Fill me with joy and gladness; let the bones which you have broken rejoice. Hide your face from my sins, and blot out all my iniquities. Create in me a clean heart, O God, and put a new and steadfast spirit within me. Cast me not away from your presence, and take not your Holy Spirit from me. Restore to me the joy of your salvation, and uphold me with a willing spirit. Then I will teach transgressors your ways, and sinners will return to you. Deliver me from blood-guiltiness, O God, the God of my salvation, and my tongue will sing aloud of your deliverance. O Lord, open my lips, and my mouth shall show forth your praise. For you have no delight in sacrifice; were I to give a burnt offering, you would not be pleased. The sacrifice acceptable to God is a broken spirit; a broken and contrite heart, O God, you will not despise. Do good to Zion in your good pleasure; rebuild the walls of Jerusalem; then you will delight in right sacrifices, in burnt offerings and whole burnt offerings; then bulls will be offered on your altar.

Then follows the Canon, in tone 4, whose acrostic is: "The Prayer of the Oil, a Song of Arsenius."

Canon

Ode 1

Hirmos: When of old Israel crossed the Red Sea without getting wet, by the cross-wise stretching forth of Moses' hands, they defeated the forces of Amalek in the wilderness.

Refrain: O merciful Lord, have mercy and heal your suffering servant.

Troparia: With the oil of mercy, O Master, you always make glad both the souls and bodies of men; with oil you preserve the faithful. Even now, with this oil show mercy on those who draw near to you.

Refrain: O merciful Lord, have mercy and heal your suffering servant.

The whole earth, O Lord, is filled with your mercy. Today we shall be anointed with your precious, divine oil; and in faith we ask you: grant us your mercy which passes all understanding.

Glory . . .

Through your apostles, O loving God, you mercifully commanded us to perform your sacred anointing upon your ailing servants. Through their prayers and through the seal of your anointing, have mercy on us all.

Now and ever . . .

Theotokion: O only Pure One, who gave birth to the boundless source of peace, by your ceaseless prayers deliver your servant from infirmities and afflictions, that he(she) may always glorify you.

Ode 3

Hirmos: In you, O Christ, the Church rejoices and cries out: "You are my fortress, O Lord, my refuge and my confirmation!"

Refrain: O merciful Lord, have mercy and heal your suffering servant.

Troparia: You alone are full of wonders! You alone are merciful to the faithful! Grant your grace from above to your ailing servant (name).

Refrain: O merciful Lord, have mercy and heal your suffering servant.

By your divine command, O Lord, of old you showed forth an olive-branch to hold back the flood; now save your suffering servant.

Glory . . .

With the lamp of your divine light, O Christ, in your mercy enlighten through anointing him(her) who in faith hastens to your mercy.

Now and ever . . .

Theotokion: Graciously look down from on high, O Mother of the Creator of all, and through your prayers deliver your suffering servant from sharp afflictions.

Kathisma Hymn (Tone 8)

You are like a divine river of mercy, an inexhaustible source of compassionate mercy, O Bountiful One. Show forth the streams of your divine mercy and heal us all; pour out abundant floods of wonders and wash us all clean: for we always have recourse to you and fervently seek your grace.

and another (Tone 4)

O Physician and Helper of the suffering, O Redeemer and Savior of the sick, O Master and Lord of all, grant healing to your ailing servant. Show compassion, have mercy on him(her) who has grievously sinned, and deliver him(her) from his(her) sins, that he(she) may glorify your divine power.

Ode 4

Hirmos: Seeing you, the Sun of Righteousness, hanging on the cross, the Church stands before you and rightly cries out: "Glory to your power, O Lord."

Refrain: O merciful Lord, have mercy and heal your suffering servant.

Troparia: Like pure chrism, O Savior, you pour out your grace and purify the world: show your divine mercy and compassion upon the bodily wounds of the one who in faith is to be anointed.

Refrain: O merciful Lord, have mercy and heal your suffering servant.

Because you seal the senses of your servant with the joy of the seal of your mercy, O Master, make him(her) impervious to all adverse powers.

Glory . . .

You commanded the sick to summon the godly ministers, to obtain salvation through their prayers and anointing with your oil: O loving God, by your mercy save your suffering servant.

Now and ever . . .

Theotokion: O all-holy, ever-virgin Theotokos, steadfast Protectress and Refuge, Haven and Wall, Ladder and Bulwark: have mercy and compassion upon this suffering servant, for to you alone has he(she) fled for refuge.

Ode 5

Hirmos: You, O my Lord, are the light that has come into the world, the light that turns from the darkness of ignorance those who with faith sing your praise.

Refrain: O merciful Lord, have mercy and heal your suffering servant.

Troparia: You are the endless source of mercy, O Good One: by your divine mercy, O Merciful One, show your mercy upon this suffering servant, for you are compassionate.

Refrain: O merciful Lord, have mercy and heal your suffering servant.

Ineffably you sealed our souls and bodies with your divine image, O Christ: heal us all by your hand.

Glory . . .

In your indescribable love, O supremely good Lord, you accepted anointment with myrrh from the sinful woman: have compassion on your servant.

Now and ever . . .

Ode 6

Hirmos: Cleansed of the blood of demons by the blood which flowed mercifully from your side, the Church cries out to you: "A sacrifice of praise will I offer you, O Lord!"

Refrain: O merciful Lord, have mercy and heal your suffering servant.

Troparia: By your words, O Loving God, you declared anointing for kings and accomplished it through priests: by your seal save also your suffering servant, for you are compassionate.

Refrain: O merciful Lord, have mercy and heal your suffering servant.

Let no bitter demons touch the senses of him(her) who is sealed with your divine anointing, O Savior, but surround him(her) with the shelter of your glory.

Glory . . .

Stretch forth your hand from on high, O God who loves mankind; and having blessed your oil, O Savior, bestow it on your servant for healing and for a release from all ills.

Now and ever . . .

Theotokion: You showed yourself to be a fruitful olive tree in the house of God, O Mother of the Creator, and through you we see the world full of mercy: by your prayers, relieve also the pangs of your suffering servant.

<hr>

Kontakion (tone 2)

O Fountain of mercy, greatly good One, deliver from every adversity these servants who adore your ineffable mercy, O compassionate One. Deliver them from all affliction, remove their diseases, and grant them divine grace from on high.

Ode 7

Hirmos: Consumed by a burning love of godliness greater than the flame, the children of Abraham in the Persian furnace cried out: "Blessed are you in the temple of your glory, O Lord!"

Refrain: O merciful Lord, have mercy and heal your suffering servant.

Troparia: In your mercy and compassion, O only God and Savior, you heal both the passions of the soul and the failings of the body: restore also this suffering servant and heal him(her).

Refrain: O merciful Lord, have mercy and heal your suffering servant.

When the heads of all are anointed with oil, grant the joy of gladness to this servant, who seeks the mercy of your redemption, O Christ, and bestow the riches of your grace, O Lord.

Glory . . .

Your seal is a sword against demons, O Savior, a fire consuming the passions of the soul through the prayers of the priest. So we, who have received healing, in faith sing praises to you.

Now and ever . . .

Theotokion: O Mother of God, in your womb you worthily contained him who holds all things in the hollow of his hand, and ineffably you gave him birth: we pray you, alleviate the suffering of this servant.

Ode 8

Hirmos: Daniel stretched out his hands and closed the jaws of the lion in the den, and the godly young men quenched the raging fire by girding themselves with virtue and crying out: "Bless the Lord, all you works of the Lord!"

Refrain: O merciful Lord, have mercy and heal your suffering servant.

Troparia: You have mercy on all, O Savior, according to your great and divine mercy. For this reason we all gather together, mystically imitating your desire for compassion and in faith bringing anointing with oil to your servant: you yourself grant him healing.

Refrain: O merciful Lord, have mercy and heal your suffering servant.

By the streams of your mercy, O Christ, and through anointing by your priests, O merciful Lord, wash away his(her) pain and hurt, and the sudden attacks of suffering caused by the violence of passions, so that he(she) may praise you with thanks, O Savior.

Let us bless the Father, the Son, and the Holy Spirit, the Lord.

Your divine mercy has been decreed from on high, O Master, as a sign of condescension and joy: do not take away your mercy, nor despise him(her) who with faith continuously cries: "Bless the Lord, all you works of the Lord!"

Now and ever . . .

Theotokion: Nature accepted your divine birthgiving, O pure one, as a glorious crown, which crushed the hosts of the enemy and defeated its dominion. Crowned, therefore, with the joyful radiance of your grace, O all-praised Lady, we sing praises to you.

Ode 9

Hirmos: From you, an unhewn mountain, O Virgin, was cut Christ, the cornerstone not cut by human hand, who united the natures that had been divided. In joy, therefore, we magnify you, O Theotokos.

Refrain: O merciful Lord, have mercy and heal your suffering servant.

Troparia: Look down from heaven, O compassionate One, and show forth your mercy upon us all. Give now your help and your strength, O God who loves mankind, to him(her) who draws near to you through divine anointing at the hands of your priests.

Refrain: O merciful Lord, have mercy and heal your suffering servant.

Rejoicing, we have seen your divine oil, which you have accepted in your divine condescension, O all-good Savior, and which you distribute as communion to those who have partaken of the divine bath.

Glory . . .

Show compassion, have mercy, O Savior, deliver from terror and pain, rescue from the arrows of the Evil One the souls and bodies of your servants: for you are a merciful Lord, who heals by your divine grace.

Now and ever . . .

Theotokion: As you receive the hymns and prayers of your servants, O Virgin, so also deliver from grievous suffering and pain him(her) who, through us, flees to your divine protection, O all-pure one.

It is truly fitting to bless you, O Theotokos, ever blessed and most pure and the Mother of our God. More honorable than the Cherubim and beyond compare more glorious than the Seraphim, without corruption you gave birth to God the Word: true Theotokos, we magnify you.

Exaposteilarion

As we gather in your holy temple to anoint your suffering servant(s) with divine oil, O good One, look with divine mercy upon our petitions.

Praises (tone 4)

Let everything that breathes praise the Lord! Praise the Lord from the heavens! Praise him in the highest! To you, O God, is due a song!

Praise him, all his angels! Praise him, all his hosts! To you, O God, is due a song!

Stichera: By this holy oil, O God who loves and forgives mankind, through your apostles you have given your grace to heal the wounds and infirmities of all. Have mercy now upon him(her) who with faith approaches your oil; in your compassion, O Lord, sanctify him(her), have mercy on him(her), cleanse him(her) from every disease, and grant him(her) your incorruptible food.

Verse: Praise him with timbrel and dance! Praise him with strings and pipe!

You are compassionate, O ineffable One; by your invisible hand, O God who loves mankind, you have sealed our senses with your divine oil. Look down from heaven upon him(her) who appeals to you in faith and asks for the forgiveness of his(her) sins. Grant healing of both soul and body, so that he(she) may glorify you and magnify your power.

Verse: Praise him with sounding cymbals! Praise him with loud clashing cymbals! Let everything that breathes praise the Lord!

By anointing with your holy oil and through the touch of priests, O God who loves mankind, from on high sanctify your servant. Free him(her) from his(her) infirmities; purge his(her) spirit. Wash him(her), O Savior, and deliver him(her) from every cunning temptation. Assuage his(her) suffering; avert all obstacles; remove all afflictions, for you are compassionate and merciful.

Glory to the Father, and to the Son, and to the Holy Spirit, now and ever, and unto ages of ages. Amen.

Theotokion: O most pure palace of the King, O greatly honored one, I pray you to cleanse my mind polluted by every sin, and to make it into an acceptable dwelling for the most-divine Trinity: so that I, your unprofitable servant, may be saved and praise your power and your infinite mercy.

READER: Holy God, Holy Mighty, Holy Immortal, have mercy on us. (3)

Glory to the Father, and to the Son, and to the Holy Spirit, now and ever and unto ages of ages. Amen.

O most holy Trinity, have mercy on us. Lord, cleanse us from our sins. Master, pardon our transgressions. Holy One, visit and heal our infirmities for your name's sake.

Lord, have mercy. (3)

Our Father, who art in heaven, hallowed be thy name. Thy kingdom come. Thy will be done, on earth as it is in heaven. Give us this day our daily bread; and forgive us our trespasses, as we forgive those who trespass against us; and lead us not into temptation, but deliver us from evil.

PRIEST: For yours is the kingdom, and the power, and the glory, of the Father, and of the Son, and of the Holy Spirit, now and ever, and unto ages of ages.

Troparion (tone 4)

You alone are a speedy helper, O Christ: speedily visit from on high your suffering servant. Deliver him(her) from diseases and acute suffering; raise him(her) up to sing praises to you and ceaselessly to glorify you, the God who alone loves mankind, through the prayers of the Theotokos.

Then the deacon, or the principal priest, recites the following litany:

Litany

DEACON: In peace, let us pray to the Lord.

PEOPLE: Lord, have mercy.

DEACON: For the peace from above, and for the salvation of our souls, let us pray to the Lord.

PEOPLE: Lord, have mercy.

DEACON: For this holy house, and for those who enter it with faith, reverence, and the fear of God, let us pray to the Lord.

PEOPLE: Lord, have mercy.

DEACON: That he will bless this oil through the power, operation, and descent of the Holy Spirit, let us pray to the Lord.

PEOPLE: Lord, have mercy.

DEACON: For the servant of God (name), that God may visit him(her), and that the grace of the Holy Spirit may come upon him(her), let us pray to the Lord.

PEOPLE: Lord, have mercy.

DEACON: That he will deliver him(her) and us from all affliction, wrath, danger, and distress, let us pray to the Lord.

PEOPLE: Lord, have mercy.

DEACON: Help us, save us, have mercy on us, and protect us, O God, by your grace.

PEOPLE: Lord, have mercy.

DEACON: Remembering our most holy, pure, most blessed and glorious Lady, the Theotokos and ever-virgin Mary, with all the saints, let us commit ourselves, and one another, and our whole life to Christ our God.

PEOPLE: To you, O Lord.

Then the principal priest recites the "Prayer of the Oil" over the vigil lamp, into which he pours some oil. In some churches, some wine is also mixed into the oil. The other priests recite the same prayer silently.

Prayer of the Oil

O Lord, in your mercy and compassion, you heal the afflictions of our souls and bodies: sanctify now this oil, O Master, that it may bring healing to those who are anointed with it, relief from every passion, from every sickness of flesh and spirit, and from all evil; and so that your holy name may be glorified, of the Father, and of the Son, and of the Holy Spirit, now and ever, and unto ages of ages.

PEOPLE: Amen.

The following troparia are sung:

Troparia

Tone 4

You alone are a speedy helper, O Christ: swiftly visit from on high your suffering servant. Deliver him(her) from disease and bitter pain; raise him(her) up to sing praises to you and ceaselessly to glorify you, the only loving God, through the prayers of the Theotokos.

Spiritually blind, O Christ, I come to you as did the man born blind, and in repentance I call out to you: "Make your light to shine upon those in darkness!"

Tone 3

My soul is paralyzed by many sins and evil deeds; yet by your divine intercession, O Lord, raise up my soul, as of old you raised the paralytic, so that being saved I may cry to you: "Grant me healing, O compassionate Christ!"

St James, tone 2

As a disciple of the Lord, O righteous James, you received the gospel; as a martyr, you have the ultimate victory; as a brother of the Lord, you have boldness; as a hierarch, you have the power of prayer: Implore Christ our God that he may save our souls.

St James, tone 4

The only-begotten Word of God the Father, who in these days has dwelt among us, appointed you, O divine James, to be the first shepherd and teacher of the church in Jerusalem, and a faithful steward of spiritual mysteries: therefore, O apostle, we all honor you.

St Nicholas, tone 3

To the people of Myra, O holy one, you showed yourself as priest: fulfilling the gospel of Christ, O holy one, you laid down your life for your people and saved the innocent from death. Therefore you are canonized as a great initiate in the grace of God.

St Demetrios, tone 3

The world has found in you a champion great in suffering, O victorious one, who put the pagans to flight. For as you humbled the pride of Lyaios and encouraged Nestor to strive for the prize, O Saint Demetrios, pray to Christ our God that he will grant us great mercy.

St Panteleimon, tone 3

O holy victor and healer Panteleimon, pray to the merciful God that he will grant our souls forgiveness of sins.

Unmercenary Saints, tone 8

O holy unmercenaries and wonderworkers, visit our infirmities. Freely you have received, freely give to us.

St John the Theologian, tone 2

Who shall declare your greatness, O virgin one? For you are rich in wonders and pour forth streams of healing. You intercede for our souls, for you are a theologian and friend of Christ.

Theotokion, tone 2

O fervent intercession and impregnable wall, O fountain of mercy and refuge of the world, fervently we call out to you: Come to our aid, O Lady; deliver us from adversity, O Theotokos, who alone are a speedy defender.

First Anointing

Prokeimenon

DEACON: Let us be attentive.

FIRST PRIEST: Peace be to all.

READER: And to your spirit.

DEACON: Wisdom.

READER: The Prokeimenon in the first tone. Let your steadfast love, O Lord, be upon us, even as we hope on you. (Ps 33[32].22)

verse: Rejoice in the Lord, O you righteous! Praise befits the upright. (Ps 33[32].1)

Epistle (James 5.10–16)

DEACON: Wisdom.

READER: The reading is from the General Epistle of St James.

DEACON: Let us be attentive.

READER: Brethren, as an example of suffering and patience, take the prophets who spoke in the name of the Lord. Behold, we call those happy who were steadfast. You have heard of the steadfastness of Job, and you have seen the purpose of the Lord, how the Lord is compassionate and merciful.

But above all, my brethren, do not swear, either by heaven or by earth or with any other oath, but let your yes be yes and your no be no, that you may not fall under condemnation.

Is any one among you suffering? Let him pray. Is any cheerful? Let him sing praise. Is any among you sick? Let him call for the elders of the church, and let them pray over him, anointing him with oil in the name of the Lord; and the prayer of faith will save the sick man, and the Lord will raise him up; and if he has committed sins, he will be forgiven. Therefore confess your sins to one another, and pray for one another, that you may be healed. The prayer of a righteous man has great power in its effects.

PRIEST: Peace be to you.

READER: And to your spirit. Alleluia, alleluia, alleluia. *(tone 8)*

PEOPLE: Alleluia, alleluia, alleluia.

READER, *verse:* I will sing of loyalty and of justice; to you, O Lord, I will sing. (Ps 101[100].1)

PEOPLE: Alleluia, alleluia, alleluia.

Gospel (Luke 10.25–37)

DEACON: Wisdom. Attend. Let us listen to the Holy Gospel.

PRIEST: Peace be to all.

PEOPLE: And to your spirit.

PRIEST: The reading is from the Holy Gospel according to Saint Luke.

PEOPLE: Glory to you, O Lord, glory to you.

DEACON: Let us be attentive.

FIRST PRIEST: At that time, a lawyer stood up to put him to the test, saying: "Teacher, what shall I do to inherit eternal life?" He said to him, "What is written in the law? How do you read?" and he answered, "You shall love the Lord your God with all your heart, and with all your soul, and with all your strength, and with all your mind; and your neighbor as yourself." And he said to him, "You have answered right; do this, and you will live."

But he, desiring to justify himself, said to Jesus, "And who is my neighbor?" Jesus replied, "A man was going down from Jerusalem to Jericho, and he fell among robbers, who stripped and beat him, and departed, leaving him half dead. Now by chance a priest was going down that road; and when he saw him he passed by on the other side. So likewise a Levite, when he came to the place and saw him, passed by on the other side. But a Samaritan, as he journeyed, came to where he was; and when he saw him, he had compassion, and went to him and bound up his wounds, pouring on oil and wine; then he set him on his own beast and brought him to an inn, and took care of him. And the next day he took out two denarii and gave them to the innkeeper, saying, 'Take care of him; and whatever more you spend, I will repay you when I come back.' Which of these, do you think, proved neighbor to the man who fell among robbers?" He said, "The one who showed mercy on him." And Jesus said to him, "Go and do likewise."

PEOPLE: Glory to you, O Lord, glory to you.

Then the deacon recites the litany:

Litany

DEACON: Have mercy on us, O God, in your great loving-kindness: we pray you, hear us, and have mercy.

PEOPLE: Lord, have mercy. (3)

DEACON: Again we pray for mercy, life, peace, health, salvation, and remission of sins of the servant of God (name).

PEOPLE: Lord, have mercy. (3)

DEACON: That he(she) may be pardoned every transgression, let us pray to the Lord.

PEOPLE: Lord, have mercy. (3)

PRIEST: For you are a merciful God who loves mankind, and to you we give glory, to the Father, and to the Son, and to the Holy Spirit, now and ever, and unto ages of ages.

PEOPLE: Amen.

Prayer

DEACON: Let us pray to the Lord.

PEOPLE: Lord, have mercy.

FIRST PRIEST: You are without beginning, eternal, holy of holies, who sent down your only-begotten Son to heal every disease and every infirmity of our souls and bodies: send down your Holy Spirit and sanctify this oil; and grant that it may bring full pardon from sin to your servant (name) who is to be anointed, and the inheritance of the kingdom of Heaven.

Some say the prayer only to here, adding the exclamation "For you are merciful and save us . . ." Others recite the prayer to the end.

For you are a great and wonderful God: you keep your covenant and your mercy toward those who love you, granting forgiveness of sins through your holy Child, Jesus Christ, who grants us a new birth from sin, who gives light to the blind, who raises up those who are cast down, who loves the righteous and shows mercy to sinners, who leads us out of darkness and the shadow of death, saying to those in chains, "Go forth," and to those who sit in darkness, "Open your eyes." You made the light of the knowledge of his countenance to shine in our hearts when for our sakes he revealed himself upon earth, and dwelt among us. To those who accepted him, he gave the power to become children of God, granting us adoption through the washing of regeneration and removing us from the tyranny of the devil. For it did not please you that we should be cleansed by blood, but by holy oil, so you gave us the image of his Cross, that we might become the flock of Christ, a royal priesthood, a holy nation; and you purified us with water and sanctified us with the Holy Spirit.

Yourself, O Master and Lord, grant us grace in this your ministry, as you gave it to Moses, your servant, to Samuel, your beloved, to John, your chosen one, and to all those who, from generation to generation, have been well-pleasing to you. So also make us to be ministers of the new covenant of your Son over this oil, which you have acquired through the precious blood of your Christ; so that putting aside our worldly desires, we may die to sin and live in righteousness, clothed in him through the anointing with the oil of sanctification which we are about to undergo.

Let this oil, O Lord, become the oil of gladness, the oil of sanctification, a royal robe, an armor of might, the averting of every work of the devil, an unassailable seal, the joy of the heart, and eternal rejoicing. Grant that those who are anointed with this oil of regeneration may be fearsome to their adversaries, and that they may shine with the radiance of your saints, having neither stain nor defect, and that they may attain your everlasting rest and receive the prize of their high calling. For you are merciful and save us, O God, our God, and to you we give glory, together with your only-begotten Son and your all-holy, good, and life-giving Spirit: now and ever, and unto ages of ages.

 Amen.

After the prayer, the priest takes one of the cotton swabs, dips it into the holy oil, and anoints the sick person, crosswise, on the brows, the nostrils, the cheeks, the lips, the breast, and on both sides of the hands. As he anoints the sick person, he recites the following prayer:

Prayer of Anointing

O holy Father, Physician of souls and bodies, who sent your only-begotten Son, our Lord Jesus Christ, who heals every infirmity and delivers from death: heal also your servant (name) from the infirmities of body and soul which afflict him(her), and enliven him(her) with the grace of your Christ; through the prayers of our most-holy Lady, the Theotokos and ever-virgin Mary; through the intercessions of the honorable, bodiless powers of heaven; through the power of the precious and life-giving cross; through the protection of the honorable, glorious prophet, forerunner, and baptist, John; of the holy, glorious, and most-blessed apostles; of the holy, glorious, victorious martyrs; of our venerable and God-bearing fathers; of the holy unmercenary physicians, Cosmas and Damian, Cyrus and John, Panteleimon and Hermolaus, Sampson and Diomedes, Photius and Anicetas; of the holy and righteous ancestors of God, Joachim and Anna; and of all the saints. For you are the fountain of healing, O our God, and to you we give glory, to the Father, and the Son, and the Holy Spirit, now and ever, and unto ages of ages. Amen.

This prayer is recited by each of the priests after he has read the gospel and the prayer, as he anoints the sick person with oil.

Second Anointing

Prokeimenon

DEACON: Let us be attentive.

SECOND PRIEST: Peace be to all.

READER: And to your spirit.

DEACON: Wisdom.

READER: The Prokeimenon in the second tone. The Lord is my strength and my song; he has become my salvation. (Ps 118[117].14)

verse: The Lord has chastened me sorely, but he has not given me over to death. (Ps 118[117].18)

Epistle (Rom 15.1–7)

DEACON: Wisdom!

READER: The reading is from the Epistle of the holy Apostle Paul to the Romans.

DEACON: Let us be attentive.

READER: Brethren, we who are strong ought to bear with the failings of the weak, and not to please ourselves; let each of us please his neighbor for his good, to edify him. For Christ did not please himself; but, as it is written, "The reproaches of those who reproached you fell on me." For whatever was written in former days was written for our instruction, that by steadfastness and by the encouragement of the scriptures we might have hope. May the God of steadfastness and encouragement grant you to live in such harmony with one another, in accord with Christ Jesus, that together you may with one voice glorify the God and Father of our Lord Jesus Christ.

Welcome one another, therefore, as Christ has welcomed you, for the glory of God.

PRIEST: Peace be to you.

READER: And to your spirit. Alleluia, alleluia, alleluia. *(tone 5)*

PEOPLE: Alleluia, alleluia, alleluia.

READER, *verse:* I will sing of your steadfast love, O Lord, for ever. (Ps 89[88].1)

PEOPLE: Alleluia, alleluia, alleluia.

Gospel (Luke 19.1–10)

DEACON: Wisdom. Attend. Let us listen to the Holy Gospel.

PRIEST: Peace be to all.

PEOPLE: And to your spirit.

PRIEST: The reading is from the Holy Gospel according to Saint Luke.

PEOPLE: Glory to you, O Lord, glory to you.

DEACON: Let us be attentive.

SECOND PRIEST: At that time, he entered Jericho and was passing through. And there was a man named Zacchaeus; he was a chief tax collector, and rich. And he sought to see who Jesus was, but could not, on account of the crowd, because he was small of stature. So he ran on ahead and climbed up into a sycamore tree to see him, for he was to pass that way. And when Jesus came to the place, he looked up and said to him, "Zacchaeus, make haste and come down; for I must stay at your house today." So he made haste and came down, and received him joyfully. And when they saw it they all murmured, "He has gone in to be the guest of a man who is a sinner." And Zacchaeus stood and said to the Lord, "Behold, Lord, the half of my goods I give to the poor; and if I have defrauded anyone of anything, I restore it fourfold." And Jesus said to him, "Today salvation has come to this house, since he also is a son of Abraham. For the Son of Man came to seek and to save the lost."

PEOPLE: Glory to you, O Lord, glory to you.

Then the deacon recites the litany:

Litany

DEACON: Have mercy on us, O God, in your great loving-kindness: we pray you, hear us, and have mercy.

PEOPLE: Lord, have mercy. (3)

DEACON: Again we pray for mercy, life, peace, health, salvation, and remission of sins of the servant of God (name).

 Lord, have mercy. (3)

DEACON: That he(she) may be pardoned every transgression, let us pray to the Lord.

PEOPLE: Lord, have mercy. (3)

PRIEST: For you are a merciful God who loves mankind, and to you we give glory, to the Father, and to the Son, and to the Holy Spirit, now and ever, and unto ages of ages.

PEOPLE: Amen.

Prayer

DEACON: Let us pray to the Lord.

PEOPLE: Lord, have mercy.

SECOND PRIEST: O great and most-high God, who are worshipped by all creatures, Fountain of wisdom, bottomless Source of goodness, boundless Sea of compassion, Master who loves mankind, God of eternity and of wonders, whom no human mind can comprehend: look down upon us and hear us, your unworthy servants, and send down the gift of your healing and forgiveness of sins wherever, in your great name, we bring this oil; and heal him(her) in the abundance of your mercy. Yea, O Lord, you are easy to be entreated; you alone are merciful and loving; you repent of our evil deeds; you know that our minds are directed toward evil even from our youth; you desire not the death of a sinner, but rather that he should turn from his wickedness and live; for the salvation of sinners you became incarnate; yet, becoming a creature for the sake of your creatures, you remained God. You have said, "I came not to call the righteous but sinners to repentance." You sought the lost sheep. Diligently you searched for the lost coin, and having found it, you said: "Him who comes to me, I will not cast out." You did not despise the sinful woman who washed your precious feet with her tears, for you said, "As often as you fall, rise up and be saved." You also said, "There is joy in heaven over one sinner who repents." Look down from the heights of your dwelling, O compassionate Master, and in this hour cover us, your sinful and unworthy servants, with the shadow of the grace of the Holy Spirit. Come and abide in your servant (name), who acknowledges his(her) sins, and who in faith draws near to you. Accept him(her) in your love for mankind, forgive him(her) if he(she) has sinned in word, deed, or thought, cleanse him(her), purify him(her) from every sin. Ever abide with him(her), protect him(her) all the remaining years of his(her) life, so that, ever walking in your commandments, he(she) may not again become an object of scorn for the devil, and so that your most-holy Name may be glorified in him(her). For you are merciful and save us, O God, our God, and to you we give glory, together with your only-begotten Son and your all-holy, good, and life-giving Spirit, now and ever, and unto ages of ages.

PEOPLE: Amen.

Having completed this prayer, the second priest anoints the sick person with oil, reciting the following prayer:

Prayer of Anointing

O holy Father, Physician of souls and bodies, who sent your only-begotten Son, our Lord Jesus Christ, who heals every infirmity and delivers from death: heal also your servant (name) from the infirmities of body and soul which afflict him(her), and enliven him(her) with the grace of your Christ; through the prayers of our most-holy Lady, the Theotokos and ever-virgin Mary; through the intercessions of the honorable, bodiless powers of heaven; through the power of the precious and life-giving Cross; through the protection of the honorable, glorious prophet, forerunner, and baptist, John; of the holy, glorious, and most-blessed apostles; of the holy, glorious, victorious martyrs; of our venerable and God-bearing fathers; of the holy unmercenary physicians, Cosmas and Damian, Cyrus and John, Panteleimon and Hermolaus, Sampson and Diomedes, Photius and Anicetas; of the holy and righteous ancestors of God, Joachim and Anna; and of all the saints. For you are the fountain of healing, O our God, and to you we give glory, to the Father, and the Son, and the Holy Spirit, now and ever, and unto ages of ages. Amen.

Third Anointing

Prokeimenon

DEACON: Let us be attentive.

THIRD PRIEST: Peace be to all.

READER: And to your spirit.

DEACON: Wisdom.

READER: The prokeimenon in the fourth tone. The Lord is my light and my salvation; whom shall I fear? (Ps 27[26].1)

Epistle (1 Cor 12.27–13.8)

DEACON: Wisdom!

READER: The reading is from the First Epistle of the holy Apostle Paul to the Corinthians.

DEACON: Let us be attentive.

READER: Brethren, you are the body of Christ and individually members of it. And God has appointed in the church first apostles, second prophets, third teachers, then workers of miracles, then healers, helpers, administrators, speakers in various kinds of tongues. Are all apostles? Are all prophets? Are all teachers? Do all work miracles? Do all possess gifts of healing? Do all speak with tongues? Do all interpret? But earnestly desire the higher gifts.

And I will show you a still more excellent way.

If I speak in the tongues of men and of angels, but have not love, I am a noisy gong or a clanging cymbal. And if I have prophetic powers, and understand all mysteries and all knowledge, and if I have all faith, so as to move mountains, but have not love, I am nothing. If I give away all I have, and if I deliver my body to be burned, but have not love, I gain nothing.

Love is patient and kind; love is not jealous or boastful; it is not arrogant or rude. Love does not insist on its own way; it is not irritable or resentful; it does not rejoice at wrong, but rejoices in the right. Love bears all things, believes all things, endures all things. Love never ends.

PRIEST: Peace be to you.

READER: And to your spirit. Alleluia, alleluia, alleluia. *(tone 2)*

PEOPLE: Alleluia, alleluia, alleluia.

READER, *verse:* In you, O Lord, do I seek refuge; let me never be put to shame. (Ps 31[30].1)

PEOPLE: Alleluia, alleluia, alleluia.

Gospel (Matt 10.1, 5–8)

DEACON: Wisdom. Attend. Let us listen to the Holy Gospel.

PRIEST: Peace be to all.

PEOPLE: And to your spirit.

PRIEST: The reading is from the Holy Gospel according to Saint Matthew.

PEOPLE: Glory to you, O Lord, glory to you.

DEACON: Let us be attentive.

THIRD PRIEST: At that time, he called to him his twelve disciples and gave them authority over unclean spirits, to cast them out, and to heal every disease and every infirmity. These twelve Jesus sent out, charging them, "Go nowhere among the Gentiles, and enter no town of the Samaritans, but go rather to the lost sheep of the house of Israel. And preach as you go, saying, 'The kingdom of heaven is at hand.' Heal the sick, raise the dead, cleanse lepers, cast out demons. You received without pay, give without pay."

PEOPLE: Glory to you, O Lord, glory to you.

Litany

DEACON: Have mercy on us, O God, in your great loving-kindness: we pray you, hear us, and have mercy.

PEOPLE: Lord, have mercy. (3)

DEACON: Again we pray for mercy, life, peace, health, salvation, and remission of sins of the servant of God (name).

PEOPLE: Lord, have mercy. (3)

DEACON: That he(she) may be pardoned every transgression, let us pray to the Lord.

PEOPLE: Lord, have mercy. (3)

PRIEST: For you are a merciful God who loves mankind, and to you we give glory, to the Father, and to the Son, and to the Holy Spirit, now and ever, and unto ages of ages.

PEOPLE: Amen.

Prayer

DEACON: Let us pray to the Lord.

PEOPLE: Lord, have mercy.

THIRD PRIEST: O Master almighty, holy King, you chastise but do not kill; you raise the fallen and restore those who are cast down; you relieve our bodily afflictions: we beg you, O our God, to direct your mercy upon this oil, and upon all who shall be anointed with it in your Name, that it may be for the healing of their souls and bodies, for purification, and for the removal of every passion, every disease and infirmity, and every defilement of body and spirit. Yea,

Lord, send down from heaven your healing power: touch the bodies; quench the fever; ease the suffering; and drive away every hidden ailment. Be the physician of your servant (name): raise him(her) up from his(her) bed of sickness, from the bed of affliction, whole and fully cured, granting him(her), through your Church, that which is well-pleasing to you and accomplishes your will. For you are merciful and save us, O God, our God, and to you we give glory, together with your only-begotten Son and your all-holy, good, and life-giving Spirit, now and ever, and unto ages of ages.

 Amen.

Having completed this prayer, the third priest anoints the sick person with oil, reciting the following prayer:

Prayer of Anointing

O holy Father, Physician of souls and bodies, who sent your only-begotten Son, our Lord Jesus Christ, who heals every infirmity and delivers from death: heal also your servant (name) from the infirmities of body and soul which afflict him(her), and enliven him(her) with the grace of your Christ; through the prayers of our most-holy Lady, the Theotokos and ever-virgin Mary; through the intercessions of the honorable, bodiless powers of heaven; through the power of the precious and life-giving cross; through the protection of the honorable, glorious prophet, forerunner, and baptist, John; of the holy, glorious, and most-blessed apostles; of the holy, glorious, victorious martyrs; of our venerable and God-bearing fathers; of the holy unmercenary physicians, Cosmas and Damian, Cyrus and John,

Panteleimon and Hermolaus, Sampson and Diomedes, Photius and Anicetas; of the holy and righteous ancestors of God, Joachim and Anna; and of all the saints.

For you are the fountain of healing, O our God, and to you we give glory, to the Father, and the Son, and the Holy Spirit, now and ever, and unto ages of ages. Amen.

Fourth Anointing

Prokeimenon

DEACON: Let us be attentive.

FOURTH PRIEST: Peace be to all.

READER: And to your spirit.

DEACON: Wisdom.

READER: The prokeimenon in the fourth tone. Incline your ear to me; answer me speedily in the day when I call! (Ps 102[101].2)

verse: Hear my prayer, O Lord; let my cry come to you! (Ps 102[101].1)

Epistle (2 Cor 6.16–7.1)

DEACON: Wisdom!

READER: The reading is from the Second Epistle of the holy Apostle Paul to the Corinthians.

DEACON: Let us be attentive.

READER: Brethren, you are the temple of the living God; as God said, "I will live in them and move among them, and I will be their God, and they shall be my people. Therefore come out from them, and be separate from them, says the

Lord, and touch nothing unclean; then I will welcome you, and I will be a father to you, and you shall be my sons and daughters, says the Lord almighty." Since we have these promises, beloved, let us cleanse ourselves from every defilement of body and spirit, and make holiness perfect in the fear of God.

PRIEST: Peace be to you.

READER: And to your spirit. Alleluia, alleluia, alleluia. *(tone 2)*

PEOPLE: Alleluia, alleluia, alleluia.

READER, *verse:* I waited patiently for the Lord; he inclined his ear to me and heard my cry. (Ps 40[39].1)

PEOPLE: Alleluia, alleluia, alleluia.

Gospel (Matt 8.14–23)

DEACON: Wisdom. Attend. Let us listen to the Holy Gospel.

PRIEST: Peace be to all.

PEOPLE: And to your spirit.

PRIEST: The reading is from the Holy Gospel according to Saint Matthew.

PEOPLE: Glory to you, O Lord, glory to you.

DEACON: Let us be attentive.

FOURTH PRIEST: At that time, when Jesus entered Peter's house, he saw his mother-in-law lying sick with a fever; he touched her hand, and the fever left her, and she arose and served him. That evening they brought to him many who were possessed with demons; and he cast out the spirits with a word, and healed all who were sick. This was to fulfill what was spoken by the prophet Isaiah, "He took our infirmities and bore our diseases." Now when Jesus saw great crowds around him, he gave orders to go over to the other side. And a scribe came up and said to him, "Teacher, I will follow you wherever you go." And Jesus said to him, "Foxes have holes, and birds of the air have nests; but the Son of Man has nowhere to lay his head." Another of his disciples said to him, "Lord, let me first go and bury my father." But Jesus said to him, "Follow me, and leave the dead to bury their own dead." And when he got into the boat, his disciples followed him.

PEOPLE: Glory to you, O Lord, glory to you.

Then the deacon recites the litany:

Litany

DEACON: Have mercy on us, O God, in your great lovingkindness: we pray you, hear us, and have mercy.

PEOPLE: Lord, have mercy. (3)

DEACON: Again we pray for mercy, life, peace, health, salvation, and remission of sins of the servant of God (name).

PEOPLE: Lord, have mercy. (3)

DEACON: That he(she) may be pardoned every transgression, let us pray to the Lord.

PEOPLE: Lord, have mercy. (3)

PRIEST: For you are a merciful God who loves mankind, and to you we give glory, to the Father, and to the Son, and to the Holy Spirit, now and ever, and unto ages of ages.

 Amen.

Prayer

 Let us pray to the Lord.

 Lord, have mercy.

 O good Lord who loves mankind, compassionate and greatly merciful, abundant in mercy and rich in goodness, Father of mercies and God of all consolation, who through the apostles has given us power to heal the infirmities of your people through oil and prayer: make this oil to be for the healing of those who are anointed with it, for relief from every disease and all sickness, for deliverance from evil of those who in hope await salvation from you. Yea, O Master, Lord, our God almighty, we entreat you to save us all. O only Physician of our souls and bodies, sanctify us all. You heal every disease: heal also your servant (name): raise him(her) up from the bed of sickness, through the mercies of your kindness; visit him(her) with your mercy and compassion; remove from him(her) every illness and infirmity; so that, having been raised up by your mighty hand, he(she) may serve you with all thanksgiving; and that we too, who now share in your ineffable love for humanity, may hymn and glorify you, for you perform great and wondrous deeds, extraordinary and glorious. For you are merciful and save us, O God, our God, and to you we give glory, together with your only-begotten Son and your all-holy, good, and life-giving Spirit: now and ever, and unto ages of ages.

 Amen.

————

Having completed this prayer, the fourth priest anoints the sick person with oil, reciting the following prayer:

Prayer of Anointing

O holy Father, Physician of souls and bodies, who sent your only-begotten Son, our Lord Jesus Christ, who heals every infirmity and delivers from death: heal also your servant (name) from the infirmities of body and soul which afflict him(her), and enliven him(her) with the grace of your Christ; through the prayers of our most-holy Lady, the Theotokos and ever-virgin Mary; through the intercessions of the honorable, bodiless powers of heaven; through the power of the precious and life-giving cross; through the protection of the honorable, glorious prophet, forerunner, and baptist, John; of the holy, glorious, and most-blessed apostles; of the holy, glorious, victorious martyrs; of our venerable and God-bearing fathers; of the holy unmercenary physicians, Cosmas and Damian, Cyrus and John, Panteleimon and Hermolaus, Sampson and Diomedes, Photius and Anicetas; of the holy and righteous ancestors of God, Joachim and Anna; and of all the saints. For you are the fountain of healing, O our God, and to you we give glory, to the Father, and the Son, and the Holy Spirit, now and ever, and unto ages of ages. Amen.

Fifth Anointing

Prokeimenon

DEACON: Let us be attentive.

FIFTH PRIEST: Peace be to all.

READER: And to your spirit.

DEACON: Wisdom.

READER: The prokeimenon in the fifth tone. Do you, O Lord, protect us, guard us ever from this generation. (Ps 12[11].7)

verse: Help, Lord; for there is no longer any that is godly. (Ps 12[11].1)

Epistle (2 Cor 1.8–11)

DEACON: Wisdom!

READER: The reading is from the Second Epistle of the holy Apostle Paul to the Corinthians.

DEACON: Let us be attentive.

READER: For we do not want you to be ignorant, brethren, of the affliction we experienced in Asia; for we were so utterly, unbearably crushed that we despaired of life itself. Why, we felt that we had received the sentence of death; but that was to make us rely not on ourselves but on God who raises the dead; he delivered us from so deadly a peril, and he will deliver us; on him we have set our hope that he will deliver us again. You also must help us by prayer, so that many will give thanks on our behalf for the blessing granted us in answer to many prayers.

PRIEST: Peace be to you.

READER: And to your spirit. Alleluia, alleluia, alleluia. *(tone 1)*

PEOPLE: Alleluia, alleluia, alleluia.

PEOPLE: Alleluia, alleluia, alleluia.

Gospel (Matt 25.1–13)

DEACON: Wisdom. Attend. Let us listen to the Holy Gospel.

PRIEST: Peace be to all.

PEOPLE: And to your spirit.

PRIEST: The reading is from the Holy Gospel according to Saint Matthew.

PEOPLE: Glory to you, O Lord, glory to you.

DEACON: Let us be attentive.

FIFTH PRIEST: The Lord spoke this parable: "Then the kingdom of heaven shall be compared to ten maidens who took their lamps and went to meet the bridegroom. Five of them were foolish, and five were wise. For when the foolish took their lamps, they took no oil with them; but the wise took flasks of oil with their lamps. As the bridegroom was delayed, they all slumbered and slept. But at midnight there was a cry, 'Behold, the bridegroom! Come out to meet him.' Then all those maidens rose and trimmed their lamps. And the foolish said to the wise, 'Give us some of your oil, for our lamps are going out.' But the wise replied, 'Perhaps there will not be enough for us and for you; go rather to the dealers and buy for yourselves.' And while they went to buy, the bridegroom came, and those who were ready went in with him to the marriage feast; and the door was shut. Afterward the other maidens came also, saying, 'Lord,

---

Lord, open to us.' But he replied, 'Truly, I say to you, I do not know you.' Watch therefore, for you know neither the day nor the hour."

PEOPLE: Glory to you, O Lord, glory to you.

Then the deacon recites the litany:

Litany

DEACON: Have mercy on us, O God, in your great loving-kindness: we pray you, hear us, and have mercy.

PEOPLE: Lord, have mercy. (3)

DEACON: Again we pray for mercy, life, peace, health, salvation, and remission of sins of the servant of God (name).

PEOPLE: Lord, have mercy. (3)

DEACON: That he(she) may be pardoned every transgression, let us pray to the Lord.

PEOPLE: Lord, have mercy. (3)

PRIEST: For you are a merciful God who loves mankind, and to you we give glory, to the Father, and to the Son, and to the Holy Spirit, now and ever, and unto ages of ages.

PEOPLE: Amen.

Prayer

DEACON: Let us pray to the Lord.

PEOPLE: Lord, have mercy.

FIFTH PRIEST: O Lord our God, you chastise and heal us again; you raise up the beggar from the earth and exalt the poor from the dunghill. O Father of orphans, Refuge of the storm-tossed, and Physician of the sick, easily you bore our diseases and took on our infirmities. Joyfully you show mercy, passing over our transgressions and taking away our unrighteousness; you are quick to help and slow to anger. You breathed on your disciples and said, "Receive the Holy Spirit: if you forgive the sins of any, they are forgiven." You accept the repentance of sinners and have authority to forgive many and grievous sins; you grant healing to all who experience weakness and prolonged illness. You have also called me, your humble, sinful, and unworthy servant, entangled in many sins and wallowing in passions, to the holy and great degree of priesthood, and to enter beyond the inner veil into the holy of holies, which the holy angels desire to approach, and to hear the voice of the Lord God, to behold the manifestation of the holy offering with my own eyes, and to take joy in the divine and sacred liturgy. Grant me the ability, as a priest, to administer your heavenly mysteries, and to offer you gifts and sacrifices for our sins, and for the ignorance of your people, and act as mediator for your reason-endowed sheep, so that you, in your great and ineffable love for humanity, may blot out their transgressions. On this holy day and at this hour, and at every time and place, O exceedingly good King, incline your ear to my prayer and receive the voice of my supplication: grant healing to your servant (name), who lies in sickness of both soul and body; grant him(her) forgiveness of his(her) sins and pardon of his(her) transgressions, both voluntary and involuntary. Heal his(her) incurable wounds, and every disease, and all infirmity. Grant healing to his(her) soul, as you touched Peter's mother-in-law, and the fever left her, and she arose and served you. Grant also healing to your servant (name), and release from all deadly suffering, O Master, remembering your abundant compassion and mercy. Remember that the human mind always inclines toward evil, even from youth, and that no one sinless is to be found upon the earth; for you alone are sinless, who came down and saved the human race and freed us from bondage to the enemy. For if you enter into judgment with your servant, no one shall be found without stain, but every mouth shall be sealed, unable to offer excuse; for before you our righteousness is like a cast-off rag. Therefore do not remember the offenses of our youth, O Lord, for you are the hope of the hopeless, the repose of those who labor and are weighed down with sin; and to you we give glory, together with your Father, who is without beginning, and your all-holy, good, and life-giving Spirit: now and ever, and unto ages of ages.

PEOPLE: Amen.

Having completed this prayer, the fifth priest anoints the sick person with oil, reciting the following prayer:

Prayer of Anointing

O holy Father, Physician of souls and bodies, who sent your only-begotten Son, our Lord Jesus Christ, who heals every infirmity and delivers from death: heal also your servant (name) from the infirmities of body and soul which afflict him(her), and enliven him(her) with the grace of your Christ; through the prayers of our most-holy Lady, the Theotokos and ever-virgin Mary; through the intercessions of the honorable, bodiless powers of heaven; through the power of the precious and life-giving cross; through the protection of the honorable, glorious prophet, forerunner, and baptist, John; of the holy, glorious, and most-blessed apostles; of the holy, glorious, victorious martyrs; of our venerable and God-bearing fathers; of the holy unmercenary physicians, Cosmas and Damian, Cyrus and John, Panteleimon and Hermolaus, Sampson and Diomedes, Photius and Anicetas; of the holy and righteous ancestors of God, Joachim and Anna; and of all the saints. For you are the fountain of healing, O our God, and to you we give glory, to the Father, and the Son, and the Holy Spirit, now and ever, and unto ages of ages. Amen.

Sixth Anointing

Prokeimenon

DEACON: Let us be attentive.

SIXTH PRIEST: Peace be to all.

READER: And to your spirit.

DEACON: Wisdom.

READER: The prokeimenon in the sixth tone. Have mercy, O Lord, according to your steadfast love. (Ps 51[50].1)

verse: Create in me a clean heart, O God, and put a new and right spirit within me. (Ps 51[50].10)

Epistle (Gal 5.22–6.2)

DEACON: Wisdom!

READER: The reading is from the Epistle of the holy Apostle Paul to the Galatians.

DEACON: Let us be attentive.

 Brethren, the fruit of the Spirit is love, joy, peace, patience, kindness, goodness, faithfulness, gentleness, self-control; against such there is no law. And those who belong to Christ have crucified the flesh with its passions and desires. If we live by the Spirit, let us also walk by the Spirit. Let us have no self-conceit, no provoking of one another, no envy of one another.

Brethren, if a man is overtaken in any trespass, you who are spiritual should restore him in a spirit of gentleness. Look to yourself, lest you too be tempted. Bear one another's burdens, and so fulfill the law of Christ.

PRIEST: Peace be to you.

READER: And to your spirit. Alleluia, alleluia, alleluia. *(tone 6)*

PEOPLE: Alleluia, alleluia, alleluia.

READER, *verse:* Blessed is the man who fears the Lord, who greatly delights in his commandments! (Ps 112[111].1)

PEOPLE: Alleluia, alleluia, alleluia.

Gospel (Matt 15.21–28)

DEACON: Wisdom. Attend. Let us listen to the Holy Gospel.

PRIEST: Peace be to all.

PEOPLE: And to your spirit.

PRIEST: The reading is from the Holy Gospel according to Saint Matthew.

PEOPLE: Glory to you, O Lord, glory to you.

DEACON: Let us be attentive.

SIXTH PRIEST: At that time, Jesus went away from there and withdrew to the district of Tyre and Sidon. And behold, a Canaanite woman from that region came out and cried, "Have mercy on me, O Lord, Son of David; my daughter is severely possessed by a demon." But he did not answer her a word. And his disciples came and begged him, saying, "Send her away, for she is crying after us." He answered, "I was sent only to the lost sheep of the house of Israel." But she came and knelt before him, saying, "Lord, help me." And he answered, "It is not fair to take the children's bread and throw it to the dogs." She said, "Yes, Lord, yet even the dogs eat the crumbs that fall from their masters' table." Then Jesus answered her, "O woman, great is your faith! Be it done for you as you desire." And her daughter was healed instantly.

PEOPLE: Glory to you, O Lord, glory to you.

Then the deacon recites the litany:

Litany

DEACON: Have mercy on us, O God, in your great loving-kindness: we pray you, hear us, and have mercy.

PEOPLE: Lord, have mercy. (3)

DEACON: Again we pray for mercy, life, peace, health, salvation, and remission of sins of the servant of God (name).

PEOPLE: Lord, have mercy. (3)

DEACON: That he(she) may be pardoned every transgression, let us pray to the Lord.

PEOPLE: Lord, have mercy. (3)

 For you are a merciful God who loves mankind, and to you we give glory, to the Father, and to the Son, and to the Holy Spirit, now and ever, and unto ages of ages.

PEOPLE: Amen.

Prayer

DEACON: Let us pray to the Lord.

PEOPLE: Lord, have mercy.

SIXTH PRIEST: We thank you, O Lord our God, who are good and love mankind, Physician of our souls and bodies, who easily bore our diseases, through whose stripes we have all been healed. O good Shepherd, you came to seek the wandering sheep; you give comfort to the faint-hearted and life to the broken-hearted; you healed the woman who for twelve years had an issue of blood; you freed the daughter of the Canaanite woman from the grievous demon; you forgave the two debtors what they owed and granted forgiveness to the sinful woman; you bestowed healing on the paralytic, as well as the forgiveness of his sins; by a word you justified the publican and accepted the thief at his last confession; you took the sins of the world and nailed them to the cross. We pray and entreat you, O God: in your goodness, loose, remit, pardon the sins and transgressions of your servant (name), voluntary or involuntary, committed in knowledge or in ignorance, by transgression or through disobedience, whether at night or by day; whether he(she) has been excommunicated by a priest, or cursed by father or mother; whether he(she) has sinned by means of sight, or of smell; through adultery, fornication, or through whatever action of body or spirit he(she) has departed from your will and your holiness. If we also have sinned in this manner, forgive us, for you are a good God, who does not remember evil and who loves humanity: do not allow him(her) or us to fall into an evil way of life, nor to follow an evil path.

Yea, O Lord and Master, at this hour hear the prayer of me, a sinner, on behalf of your servant (name), and overlook all his(her) transgressions, for you are a God who does not remember evil. Deliver him(her) from eternal punishment; fill his(her) mouth with your praise; open his(her) lips that he(she) may glorify your holy Name; stretch forth his(her) hands so that he(she) may fulfill your commandments. Guide his(her) feet aright in the way of your gospel, by your grace strengthening all his(her) members and thoughts. For you are our God, who through your holy apostles gave us a command, saying: "Whatever you bind on earth shall be bound in heaven, and whatever you loose on earth shall be loosed in heaven." And again: "If you forgive the sins of any, they are forgiven; if you retain the sins of any, they are retained." As you heard Ezekiel in the sorrow of his soul, at the hour of his death, and despised not his supplications, so also at this hour give ear to me, your humble, sinful, and unworthy servant. For you are the Lord Jesus Christ who, in your goodness and love for humanity, commanded us to forgive sinners even seventy times seven, and who repents of our wickedness and rejoices over the conversion of those who have gone astray. For as is your majesty, so also is your mercy, and to you we give glory, together with your Father, who is without beginning, and your all-holy, good, and life-giving Spirit: now and ever, and unto ages of ages.

PEOPLE: Amen.

Having completed this prayer, the sixth priest anoints the sick person with oil, reciting the following prayer:

Prayer of Anointing

O holy Father, Physician of souls and bodies, who sent your only-begotten Son, our Lord Jesus Christ, who heals every infirmity and delivers from death: heal also your servant (name) from the infirmities of body and soul which afflict him(her), and enliven him(her) with the grace of your Christ; through the prayers of our most-holy Lady, the Theotokos and ever-virgin Mary; through the intercessions of the honorable, bodiless powers of heaven; through the power of the precious and life-giving cross; through the protection of the honorable, glorious prophet, forerunner, and baptist, John; of the holy, glorious, and most-blessed apostles; of the holy, glorious, victorious martyrs; of our venerable and God-bearing fathers; of the holy unmercenary physicians, Cosmas and Damian, Cyrus and John, Panteleimon and Hermolaus, Sampson and Diomedes, Photius and Anicetas; of the holy and righteous ancestors of God, Joachim and Anna; and of all the saints. For you are the fountain of healing, O our God, and to you we give glory, to the Father, and the Son, and the Holy Spirit, now and ever, and unto ages of ages. Amen.

Seventh Anointing

Prokeimenon

DEACON: Let us be attentive.

SEVENTH PRIEST: Peace be to all.

READER: And to your spirit.

DEACON: Wisdom.

READER: The prokeimenon in the seventh tone. O Lord, rebuke me not in your anger, nor chasten me in your wrath. (Ps 6.1)

verse: Be gracious to me, O Lord, for I am languishing. (Ps 6.2)

Epistle (1 Thess 5.14–23)

DEACON: Wisdom!

READER: The reading is from the First Epistle of the holy Apostle Paul to the Thessalonians.

DEACON: Let us be attentive.

READER: We exhort you, brethren, admonish the idlers, encourage the fainthearted, help the weak, be patient with them all. See that none of you repays evil for evil, but always seek to do good to one another and to all. Rejoice always, pray constantly, give thanks in all circumstances; for this is the will of God in Christ Jesus for you. Do not quench the Spirit, do not despise prophesying, but test everything; hold fast to what is good, abstain from every form of evil.

May the God of peace himself sanctify you wholly; and may your spirit and soul and body be kept sound and blameless at the coming of our Lord Jesus Christ.

PRIEST: Peace be to you.

READER: And to your spirit. Alleluia, alleluia, alleluia. *(tone 7)*

PEOPLE: Alleluia, alleluia, alleluia.

READER, *verse:* The Lord answer you in the day of trouble! The name of the God of Jacob protect you! (Ps 20[19].1)

PEOPLE: Alleluia, alleluia, alleluia.

Gospel (Matt 9.9–13)

DEACON: Wisdom. Attend. Let us listen to the Holy Gospel.

PRIEST: Peace be to all.

PEOPLE: And to your spirit.

PRIEST: The reading is from the Holy Gospel according to Saint Matthew.

PEOPLE: Glory to you, O Lord, glory to you.

DEACON: Let us be attentive.

SEVENTH PRIEST: At that time, as Jesus passed on from there, he saw a man called Matthew sitting at the tax office; and he said to him, "Follow me." And he rose and followed him. And as he sat at table in the house, behold, many tax collectors and sinners came and sat down with Jesus and his disciples. And when the Pharisees saw this, they said to his disciples, "Why does your teacher eat with tax collectors and sinners?" But when he heard it, he said, "Those who are well have no need of a physician, but those who are sick. Go and learn what this means, 'I desire mercy, and not sacrifice.' For I came not to call the righteous, but sinners."

PEOPLE: Glory to you, O Lord, glory to you.

Then the deacon recites the litany:

Litany

DEACON: Have mercy on us, O God, in your great loving-kindness: we pray you, hear us, and have mercy.

PEOPLE: Lord, have mercy. (3)

DEACON: Again we pray for mercy, life, peace, health, salvation, and remission of sins of the servant of God (name).

PEOPLE: Lord, have mercy. (3)

DEACON: That he(she) may be pardoned every transgression, let us pray to the Lord.

PEOPLE: Lord, have mercy. (3)

PRIEST: For you are a merciful God who loves mankind, and to you we give glory, to the Father, and to the Son, and to the Holy Spirit, now and ever, and unto ages of ages.

PEOPLE: Amen.

Prayer

DEACON: Let us pray to the Lord.

PEOPLE: Lord, have mercy.

SEVENTH PRIEST: O Master, Lord our God, Physician of souls and bodies, you cure chronic illnesses and heal every disease and every infirmity among the people; you desire that all should be saved and come to the knowledge of the truth; you desire not the death of the sinner, but that he should repent and live. For you, O Lord, in the old covenant appointed repentance for sinners, for David and the Ninevites, and for those who went before them. Likewise, in the dispensation of your coming in the flesh, you called not the righteous but sinners to repentance; you accepted the repentance of the publican, the harlot, the thief, and of Paul, the great blasphemer and persecutor; you accepted the repentance of Peter, your first apostle, who thrice denied you, and you declared to him: "You are Peter, and on this rock I will build my church, and the gates of Hades shall not prevail against it. I will give you the keys of the kingdom of heaven." Because of your faithful promise, O good One who loves mankind, we too have boldness, and at this hour we pray you and ask: Hear our prayer, receive it as incense offered before you; visit your servant (name). If he(she) has sinned in word, or deed, or thought, at night or by day; if he(she) has been excommunicated by a priest, or come under anathema; if he(she) has been embittered by an oath or cursed himself(herself)—we pray and entreat you: Loose, pardon, and forgive him(her), O God, overlooking his(her) sins and transgressions, committed both knowingly and unknowingly. If he(she) has transgressed your commandments, or has sinned because he(she) bears flesh and dwells in the world, or through the wiles of the devil, forgive him(her), for you are a good God and you love mankind; for there is no man who lives and does not sin. You alone are sinless, and your righteousness endures for ever, and your word is truth. You have created humanity

not for perdition, but for the keeping of your commandments and the inheritance of eternal life. And to you we give
glory, together with the Father and the Holy Spirit, now
and ever, and unto ages of ages.

PEOPLE: Amen.

*Having completed this prayer, the seventh priest anoints the sick
person with oil, reciting the following prayer:*

Prayer of Anointing

O holy Father, Physician of souls and bodies, who sent your
only-begotten Son, our Lord Jesus Christ, who heals every
infirmity and delivers from death: heal also your servant
(name) from the infirmities of body and soul which afflict
him(her), and enliven him(her) with the grace of your
Christ; through the prayers of our most-holy Lady, the
Theotokos and ever-virgin Mary; through the intercessions
of the honorable, bodiless powers of heaven; through the
power of the precious and life-giving cross; through the
protection of the honorable, glorious prophet, forerunner,
and baptist, John; of the holy, glorious, and most-blessed
apostles; of the holy, glorious, victorious martyrs; of our
venerable and God-bearing fathers; of the holy unmercenary physicians, Cosmas and Damian, Cyrus and John,
Panteleimon and Hermolaus, Sampson and Diomedes,
Photius and Anicetas; of the holy and righteous ancestors
of God, Joachim and Anna; and of all the saints. For you
are the fountain of healing, O our God, and to you we give
glory, to the Father, and the Son, and the Holy Spirit, now
and ever, and unto ages of ages. Amen.

Prayer of Absolution

After the anointing, the clergy gather around the sick person. The first priest takes the gospel book, opens it, and places it, with the writing down, on the head of the sick person, with all the priests holding the book. The first priest, who does not place his hand on the gospel, recites the following prayer:

O holy King, compassionate and of great mercy, Lord Jesus Christ, Son and Word of the living God, you desire not the death of a sinner, but that he should repent and live: it is not my sinful hand that I lay upon the head of him(her) who approaches you in sin and asks, through us, for the forgiveness of his(her) sins; but it is your strong and mighty hand, which is in this, your holy gospel, held by my fellow-ministers over the head of your servant (name). With them, I also pray and entreat your merciful love for humanity, which remembers not evil, O God our Savior, who through your prophet Nathan granted forgiveness of sins to the penitent David, and who accepted Manasses' prayer of repentance: in your customary love for humanity, accept also this your servant (name), who repents of his(her) own sins, and overlook his(her) transgressions. For you are our God, who commanded us to forgive those who fall into sin, even unto seventy times seven. For as is your majesty, so also is your mercy, and to you belong all glory, honor, and worship, now and ever, and unto ages of ages. Amen.

They remove the gospel book from the head of the sick person and present it to him(her) to kiss.

Then the deacon recites the litany:

Litany

DEACON: Have mercy on us, O God, in your great loving-kindness: we pray you, hear us, and have mercy.

PEOPLE: Lord, have mercy. (3)

DEACON: Again we pray for mercy, life, peace, health, salvation, and remission of sins of the servant of God (name).

PEOPLE: Lord, have mercy. (3)

DEACON: That he(she) may be pardoned every transgression, let us pray to the Lord.

PEOPLE: Lord, have mercy. (3)

PRIEST: For you are a merciful God who loves mankind, and to you we give glory, to the Father, and to the Son, and to the Holy Spirit, now and ever, and unto ages of ages.

PEOPLE: Amen.

Troparia

The choir sings the following troparia, in tone 4.

Glory . . .

You have a fountain of healing, O holy unmercenaries; you grant healing to all who ask, for you have been accounted worthy of very great gifts by our Savior, the ever-flowing source. For the Lord has said to you, whose zeal equals that of the apostles: Behold, I have given you power over the unclean spirits, to cast them out, and to heal every sickness and every infirmity. For nobly you have lived, according to his commandments; freely you have received, freely give, healing the diseases of our souls and bodies.

Now and ever . . .

Theotokion: Regard the prayers of your servants, O all-pure One, for you stem the fierce attacks upon us and release us from all afflictions. You alone do we have as our anchor sure and strong, and we are under your protection. When we call on you, O Lady, we shall not be put to shame. Make haste to the petitions of those who cry to you in faith: Hail, O Lady, help of all, the joy, refuge, and salvation of our souls!

Dismissal

CHOIR: Glory to the Father, and to the Son, and to the Holy Spirit, now and ever, and unto ages of ages. Amen.

Lord, have mercy. (3) Father bless.

PRIEST: May Christ our true God, through the prayers of his most-pure Mother, through the power of the precious and life-giving cross, of the holy, glorious, praiseworthy Apostle James, the first bishop of Jerusalem and brother of God, and of all the saints, save us and have mercy on us, for he is good and loves humanity.

And the person who has received anointing bows, saying:

Bless me, holy fathers, and pardon me, a sinner. (3)

And having received their blessing and pardon, he(she) goes out, giving thanks to God.

70

An Abbreviated Rite of Anointing[1]

A small table is prepared, and on it is placed a bowl of wheat and a gospel book. An empty vigil lamp is set on the wheat, and a cotton swab for anointing is placed in the wheat surrounding the lamp. Two containers, one with olive oil, the other with water (or red wine), are also placed next to it. The presbyter stands before the table, vested in his epitrachilion and phelonion and holding a candle. The priest incenses three times around the table, then the entire church or house, and the people. Then he stands before the table, facing east, and begins, saying:

PRIEST: Blessed is our God, always, now and ever, and unto ages of ages.

READER: Amen. Holy God, Holy Mighty, Holy Immortal, have mercy on us. (3) Glory to the Father, and to the Son, and to the Holy Spirit, now and ever and unto ages of ages. Amen. O most holy Trinity, have mercy on us. Lord, cleanse us from our sins. Master, pardon our transgressions. Holy One, visit and heal our infirmities for your name's sake.

Lord, have mercy. (3)

Our Father, who art in heaven, hallowed be thy name. Thy kingdom come. Thy will be done, on earth as it is in heaven. Give us this day our daily bread; and forgive us our

---

[1]This abbreviated rite is intended for emergency use in a hospital or at home. It is based on a typical adaptation found in a 14th–15th-century Slavic manuscript (*Moscow Theological Academy no. 85*, ff 242–49), described by A. Golubtsov, "Ob obriadovoi storone tainstva eleosviashcheniia," 118.

trespasses, as we forgive those who trespass against us; and lead us not into temptation, but deliver us from evil.

PRIEST: For yours is the kingdom, and the power, and the glory of the Father, and of the Son, and of the Holy Spirit, now and ever, and unto ages of ages.

Then the troparia are sung:

Have mercy on us, O Lord, have mercy on us. For we sinners, void of all defense, offer to you, as to our Master, this petition: Have mercy on us.

Glory . . .

Have mercy on us, O Lord, for in you have we trusted, and do not be very angry with us, nor remember our iniquities. But look down even now on us, for you are of tender compassion, and deliver us from our enemies. For you are our God, and we are your people. We are all the work of your hand, and we call on your name.

Now and ever . . .

Open to us the door of your loving-kindness, O blessed Theotokos. Because we have set our hope on you, may we not fail, but through you may we be delivered from all adversities: for you are the salvation of all Christians.

Then the deacon, or the principal priest, recites the following litany:

Litany

DEACON: In peace, let us pray to the Lord.

PEOPLE: Lord, have mercy.

DEACON: For the peace from above, and for the salvation of our souls, let us pray to the Lord.

PEOPLE: Lord, have mercy.

DEACON: For this holy house, and for those who enter it with faith, reverence, and the fear of God, let us pray to the Lord.

PEOPLE: Lord, have mercy.

DEACON: That he will bless this oil through the power, operation, and descent of the Holy Spirit, let us pray to the Lord.

PEOPLE: Lord, have mercy.

DEACON: For the servant of God (name), that God may visit him(her), and that the grace of the Holy Spirit may come upon him(her), let us pray to the Lord.

PEOPLE: Lord, have mercy.

DEACON: That he will deliver him(her) and us from all affliction, wrath, danger, and distress, let us pray to the Lord.

PEOPLE: Lord, have mercy.

DEACON: Help us, save us, have mercy on us, and protect us, O God, by your grace.

PEOPLE: Lord, have mercy.

DEACON: Remembering our most holy, pure, most blessed and glorious Lady, the Theotokos and ever-virgin Mary, with all the saints, let us commit ourselves, and one another, and our whole life to Christ our God.

PEOPLE: To you, O Lord.

Prayer of the Oil

O Lord, in your mercy and compassion, you heal the afflictions of our souls and bodies: sanctify now this oil, O Master, that it may bring healing to those who are anointed with it, relief from every passion, from every sickness of flesh and spirit, and from all evil; and so that your holy name may be glorified, of the Father, and of the Son, and of the Holy Spirit, now and ever, and unto ages of ages.

PEOPLE: Amen.

Prokeimenon

DEACON: Let us be attentive.

FIRST PRIEST: Peace be to all.

READER: And to your spirit.

DEACON: Wisdom.

READER: The Prokeimenon in the first tone. Let your steadfast love, O Lord, be upon us, even as we hope on you. (Ps 33[32].22)

verse: Rejoice in the Lord, O you righteous! Praise befits the upright. (Ps 33[32].1)

Epistle (James 5.10–16)

DEACON: Wisdom.

READER: The reading is from the General Epistle of St James.

DEACON: Let us be attentive.

READER: Brethren, as an example of suffering and patience, take the prophets who spoke in the name of the Lord. Behold, we call those happy who were steadfast. You have heard of the steadfastness of Job, and you have seen the purpose of the Lord, how the Lord is compassionate and merciful. But above all, my brethren, do not swear, either by heaven or by earth or with any other oath, but let your yes be yes and your no be no, that you may not fall under condemnation. Is any one among you suffering? Let him pray. Is any cheerful? Let him sing praise. Is any among you sick? Let him call for the elders of the church, and let them pray over him, anointing him with oil in the name of the Lord; and the prayer of faith will save the sick man, and the Lord will raise him up; and if he has committed sins, he will be forgiven. Therefore confess your sins to one another, and pray for one another, that you may be healed. The prayer of a righteous man has great power in its effects.

PRIEST: Peace be to you.

READER: And to your spirit. Alleluia, alleluia, alleluia. *(tone 8)*

PEOPLE: Alleluia, alleluia, alleluia.

READER, *verse:* I will sing of loyalty and of justice; to you, O Lord, I will sing. (Ps 101[100].1)

PEOPLE: Alleluia, alleluia, alleluia.

Gospel (John 5.2–24)

DEACON: Wisdom. Attend. Let us listen to the Holy Gospel.

PRIEST: Peace be to all.

PRIEST: The reading is from the Holy Gospel according to Saint John.

PEOPLE: Glory to you, O Lord, glory to you.

DEACON: Let us be attentive.

PRIEST: Now there is in Jerusalem by the Sheep Gate a pool, in Hebrew called Bethesda, which has five porticoes. In these lay a multitude of invalids, blind, lame, paralyzed. One man was there, who had been ill for thirty-eight years. When Jesus saw him and knew that he had been lying there a long time, he said to him, "Do you want to be healed?" The sick man answered him, "Sir, I have no man to put me into the pool when the water is troubled, and while I am going another steps down before me." Jesus said to him, "Rise, take up your pallet, and walk." And at once the man was healed, and he took up his pallet and walked.

Now that day was the Sabbath. So the Jews said to the man who was cured, "It is the Sabbath, it is not lawful for you to carry your pallet." But he answered them, "The man who healed me said to me, 'Take up your pallet, and walk.'" They asked him, "Who is the man who said to you, 'Take up your pallet, and walk'?" Now the man who had been healed did not know who it was, for Jesus had withdrawn, as there was a crowd in the place. Afterward, Jesus found him in the temple, and said to him, "See, you are well! Sin no more, that nothing worse befall you." The man went away and told the Jews that it was Jesus who had healed him. And this was why the Jews persecuted Jesus, because he did this on the Sabbath. But Jesus answered them, "My Father is working still, and I am working." This was why the Jews sought all the more to kill him, because he not only broke the Sabbath but also called God his Father, making himself equal with God.

Jesus said to them, "Truly, truly, I say to you, the Son can do nothing of his own accord, but only what he sees the Father doing; for whatever he does, that the Son does likewise. For the Father loves the Son, and shows him all that he himself is doing; and greater works than these will he show him, that you may marvel. For as the Father raises the dead and gives them life, so also the Son gives life to whom he will. The Father judges no one, but has given all judgment to the Son, that all may honor the Son, even as they honor the Father. He who does not honor the Son does not honor the Father who sent him. Truly truly, I say to you, he who hears my word and believes him who sent me, has eternal life; he does not come into judgment, but has passed from death to life."

PEOPLE: Glory to you, O Lord, glory to you.

Prayer of Anointing

O holy Father, Physician of souls and bodies, who sent your only-begotten Son, our Lord Jesus Christ, who heals every infirmity and delivers from death: heal also your servant (name) from the infirmities of body and soul which afflict him(her), and enliven him(her) with the grace of your Christ; through the prayers of our most-holy Lady, the Theotokos and ever-virgin Mary; through the intercessions of the honorable, bodiless powers of heaven; through the power of the precious and life-giving cross; through the protection of the honorable, glorious prophet, forerunner, and baptist, John; of the holy, glorious, and most-blessed apostles; of the holy, glorious, victorious martyrs; of our venerable and God-bearing fathers; of the holy unmercenary physicians, Cosmas and Damian, Cyrus and John, Panteleimon and Hermolaus, Sampson and Diomedes, Photius and Anicetas; of the holy and righteous ancestors of God, Joachim and Anna; and of all the saints. For you are the fountain of healing, O our God, and to you we give glory, to the Father, and the Son, and the Holy Spirit, now and ever, and unto ages of ages. Amen.

After the prayer, the priest takes one of the cotton swabs, dips it into the holy oil, and anoints the sick person, crosswise, on the brows, the nostrils, the cheeks, the lips, the breast, and on both sides of the hands. As he anoints the sick person, he recites the following prayer:

O good God who loves mankind, compassionate and greatly merciful, abundant in mercy and rich in goodness, Father of mercies and God of all consolation, who through the apostles has given us power to heal the infirmities of your people through oil and prayer: make this oil to be for the healing of those who are anointed with it, for relief from every disease and all sickness, for deliverance from evil of those who in hope await salvation from you. Yea, O Master, Lord, our God almighty, we entreat you to save us all. O only Physician of our souls and bodies, sanctify us all. You heal every disease; heal also your servant (name): raise him(her) up from the bed of sickness, through the mercies of your kindness; visit him(her) with your mercy and compassion; remove from him(her) every illness and infirmity;

so that, having been raised up by your mighty hand, he(she) may serve you with all thanksgiving; and that we too, who now share in your ineffable love for humanity, may hymn and glorify you, for you perform great and wondrous deeds, extraordinary and glorious. For you are merciful and save us, O God, our God, and to you we give glory, together with your only-begotten Son and your all-holy, good, and life-giving Spirit: now and ever, and unto ages of ages.

PEOPLE: Amen.

Then the deacon recites the litany:

Litany

DEACON: Have mercy on us, O God, in your great loving-kindness: we pray you, hear us, and have mercy.

PEOPLE: Lord, have mercy. (3)

DEACON: Again we pray for mercy, life, peace, health, salvation, and remission of sins of the servant of God [name].

PEOPLE: Lord, have mercy. (3)

DEACON: That he(she) may be pardoned every transgression, let us pray to the Lord.

PEOPLE: Lord, have mercy. (3)

PRIEST: For you are a merciful God who loves mankind, and to you we give glory, to the Father, and to the Son, and to the Holy Spirit, now and ever, and unto ages of ages.

PEOPLE: Amen.

Dismissal

PEOPLE: Glory to the Father, and to the Son, and to the Holy Spirit, now and ever, and unto ages of ages. Amen.

Lord, have mercy. (3) Father bless.

PRIEST: May Christ our true God, through the prayers of his most-pure Mother, through the power of the precious and life-giving cross, of the holy, glorious, praiseworthy Apostle James, the first bishop of Jerusalem and brother of God, and of all the saints, save us and have mercy on us, for he is good and loves mankind.

PEOPLE: Amen.